Cause Effect Chaos!

Planet Earth

Author Paul Mason
with artwork by Mark Ruffle

Enslow PUBLISHING

The website addresses (URLs) included in this book were valid at the time of going to press. However, it is possible that contents or addresses may have changed since the publication of this book. No responsibility for any such change can be accepted by either the author or the Publisher.

Published in 2026 by Enslow Publishing, LLC
2544 Clinton Street
Buffalo, NY 14224

First published in Great Britain in 2018 by Wayland

Series editor: Paul Rockett
Series design and illustration: Mark Ruffle
www.rufflebrothers.com

Manufactured in the United States of America

CPSIA compliance information: Batch #CSENS26: For further information contact Enslow Publishing LLC, New York, New York at 1-800-398-2504.

Please visit our website, www.enslowpublishing.com. For a free color catalog of all our high-quality books, call toll free 1-800-398-2504 or fax 1-877-980-4454.

Cataloging-in-Publication Data
Names: Mason, Paul. | Ruffle, Mark, illustrator.
Title: Planet Earth / Paul Mason ; illustrated by Mark Ruffle.
Description: Buffalo, NY : Enslow Publishing, 2026. | Series: Cause, effect, chaos! | Includes glossary and index.
Identifiers: ISBN 9781978545328 (pbk.) | ISBN 9781978545335 (library bound) | ISBN 9781978545342 (ebook)
Subjects: LCSH: Earth sciences--Juvenile literature. | Natural disasters--Juvenile literature.
Classification: LCC QE29.M376 2026 | DDC 550--dc23

Contents

Cause and Effect

What is cause and effect? It is the connection between two events, when the first event leads to the second.

One way to explain cause and effect is through examples.

Cause:
Your cousin loves singing along to pop songs. This causes her to …

Effect:

… sign up to audition for a TV talent show.

The effect of this could be that she becomes the new Queen of Pop!

But cause and effect doesn't always work out well …

Because she always wears headphones, your cousin hasn't re-alized that she can't actually sing.

The effect is embarrassment all around.

Embarrassing yourself at an audition is upsetting but not a catastrophe.

In the big processes on **planet Earth**, though, cause and effect can sometimes lead to chaos!

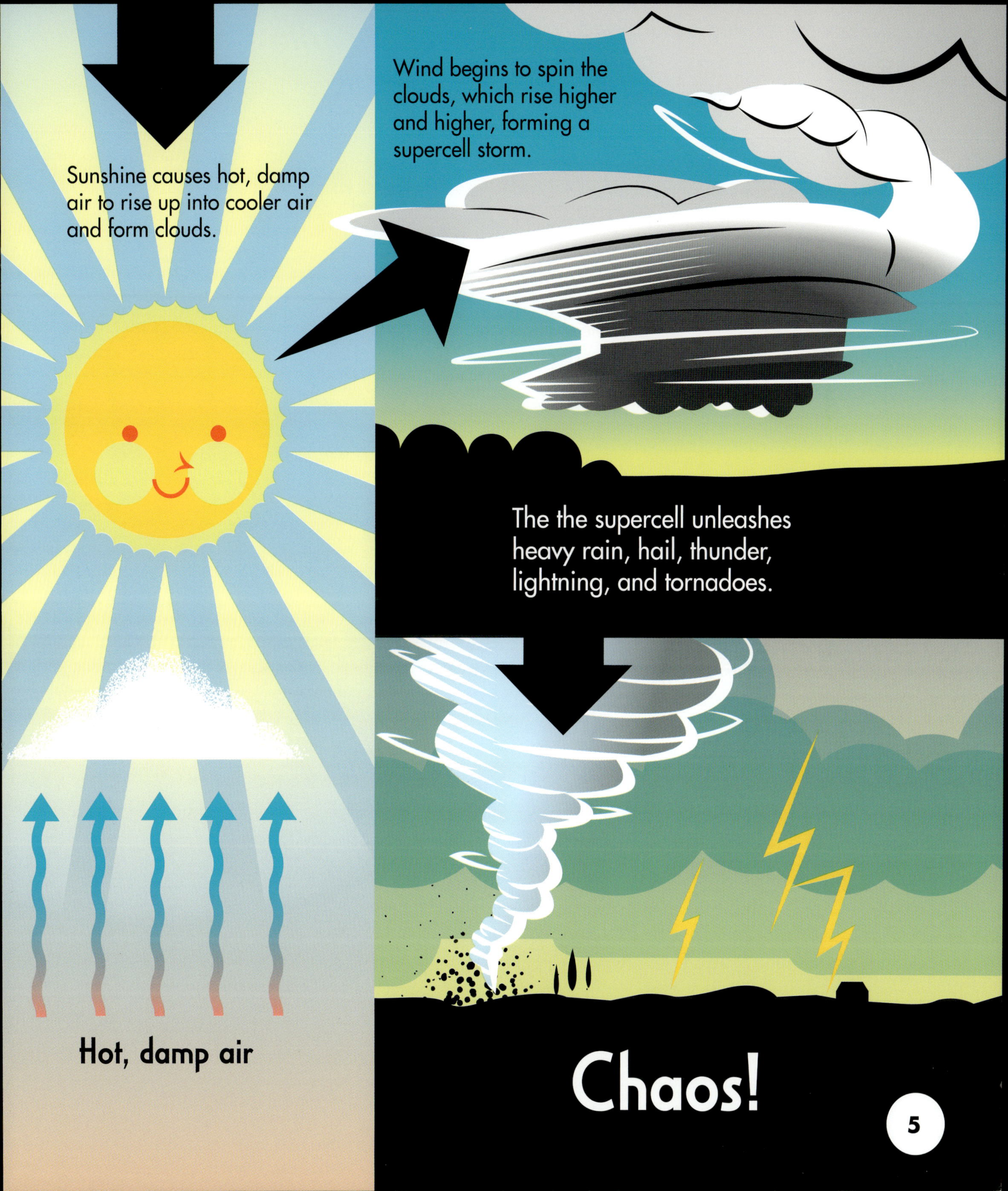

Sunshine causes hot, damp air to rise up into cooler air and form clouds.

Hot, damp air

Wind begins to spin the clouds, which rise higher and higher, forming a supercell storm.

The the supercell unleashes heavy rain, hail, thunder, lightning, and tornadoes.

Chaos!

The Big Bang

Planet Earth is an amazing, complicated, beautiful place. It's filled with roaring oceans and raging rivers, monstrous mountains, and parched deserts.

But how did the Earth come to be here in the first place?

It all started with a big bang. In fact,

***THE* Big Bang.**

The Big Bang scattered matter throughout the universe.

Among this matter was what would eventually become Earth.

The start-up Earth had enough gravity to attract more matter, in a process called

accretion.

Once Earth had reached a certain size, it began to cool on the outside. The cooling-down created a hard shell, or crust. Beneath the crust was molten matter.

As far as scientists know, out of millions of planets in the universe only Earth supports life. Imagine if things hadn't happened just as they did …

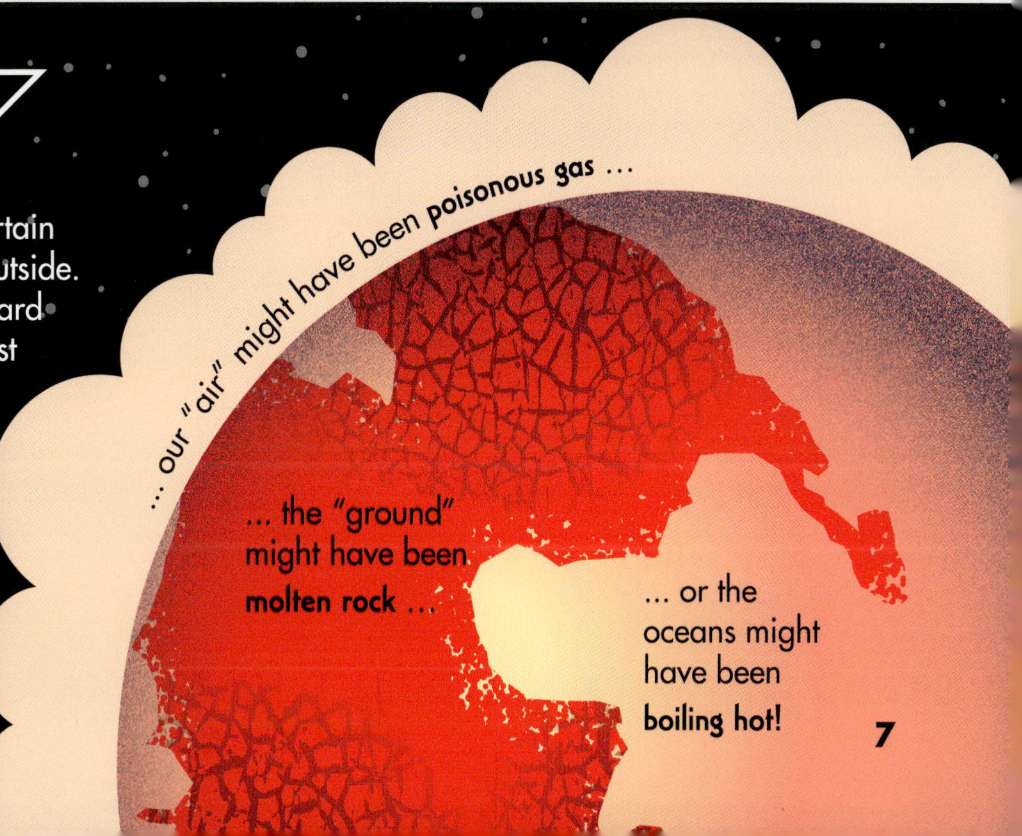

Volcanic Eruption!

Planet Earth's outer crust isn't in one piece like an egg shell. It's made of several pieces– more like a boiled egg you accidentally dropped.

The pieces are called tectonic plates. Where they meet, volcanic eruptions can happen without warning.

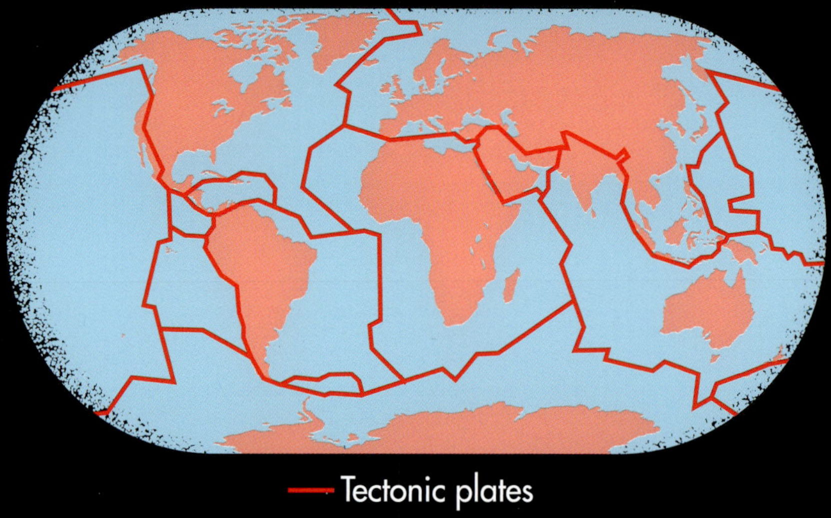

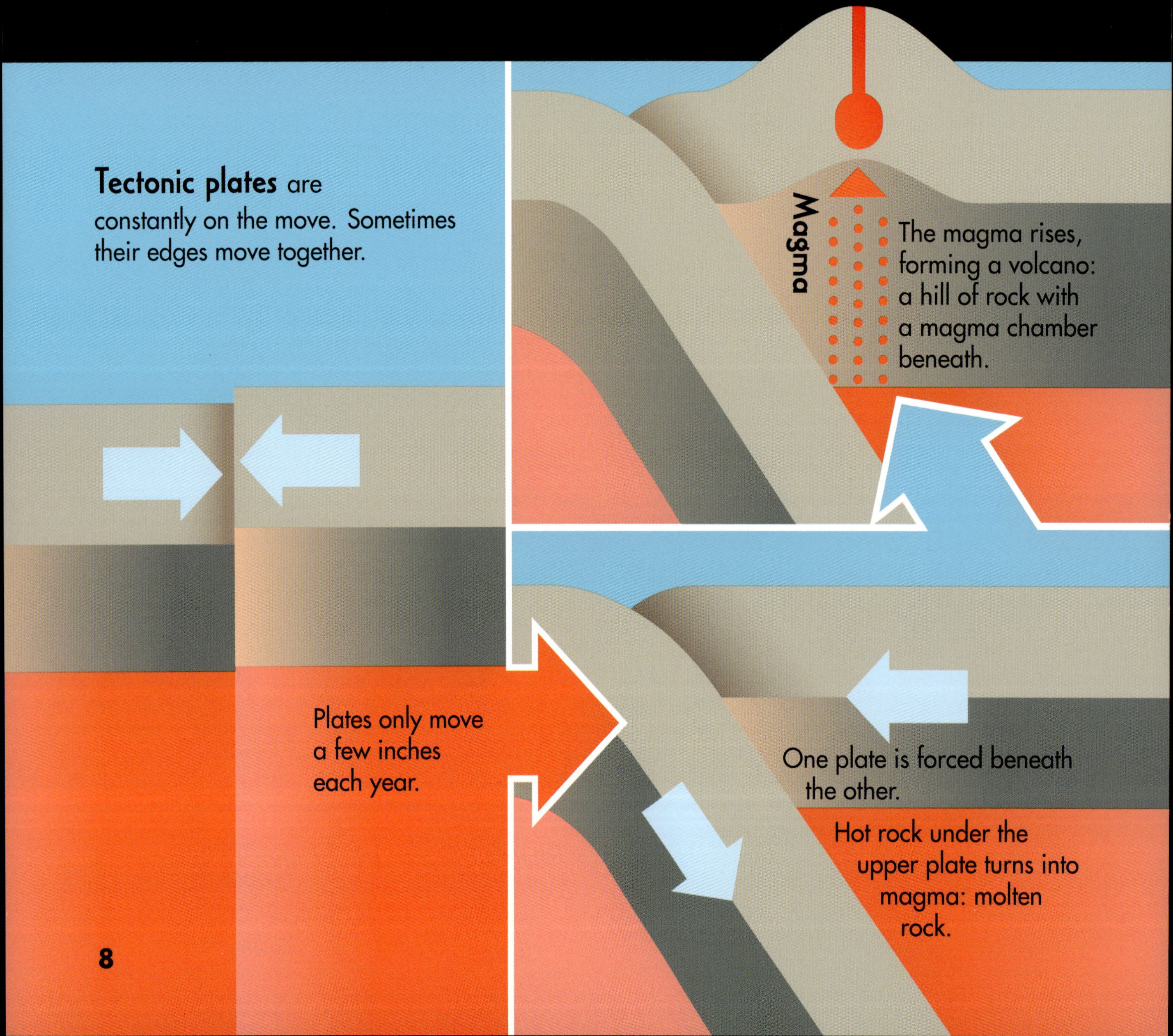

Over time, gases build up in the magma chamber, like a shaken-up soda.

When the pressure inside gets too great, the volcano erupts.

Chaos!

When Mount Vesuvius erupted in 79 CE, it **destroyed** the ancient Roman cities, Herculaneum and Pompeii.

Birth of an Island

Far out in the Pacific Ocean are the Hawaiian Islands. They are 2,330 miles (3,750 km) from North America and 3,980 miles (6,400 km) from Asia. It's a long way to the nearest continent.

The Hawaiian Islands did not float away from one of these big landmasses–so how did they get there?

Hawaii started life at a "hot spot": a place where hot matter from deep within Earth rises close to the outer crust.

Scientists think hot spots may be a cooling system for Earth's core.

The hot spot is below the ocean's tectonic-plate floor. When it gets especially hot, it melts the plate. A volcano is born, deep beneath the sea.

The volcano rises up and up, until it bursts out at the ocean surface, 3.1 miles (5 km) above.

Mauna Loa, on Hawaii, is the world's tallest volcano:

it is over 5.5 miles (9 km) high.

With its heat released, the volcano-making eruption stops–until next time.

By then, the Pacific plate will have moved.

A new island will be formed.

Hawaii's volcanoes are still **active.** They regularly erupt.

Lava flows across roads and through fields ...

buildings are destroyed ...

and clouds of ash coat the land.

Earthquake!

Mid-afternoon on May 22, 1960, in Valdivia, Chile, the ground started to shake in a violent earthquake. The city's people evacuated their buildings–but it was just a foreshock.

Thirty minutes later, the biggest earthquake ever recorded struck Chile. What caused it?

The earthquake began off the coast, where two tectonic plates were grinding against each other.

Instead of gliding smoothly, the edges of the plates had become stuck.

The **tension** between the plates kept increasing. Finally, they began to release, causing a series of foreshocks.

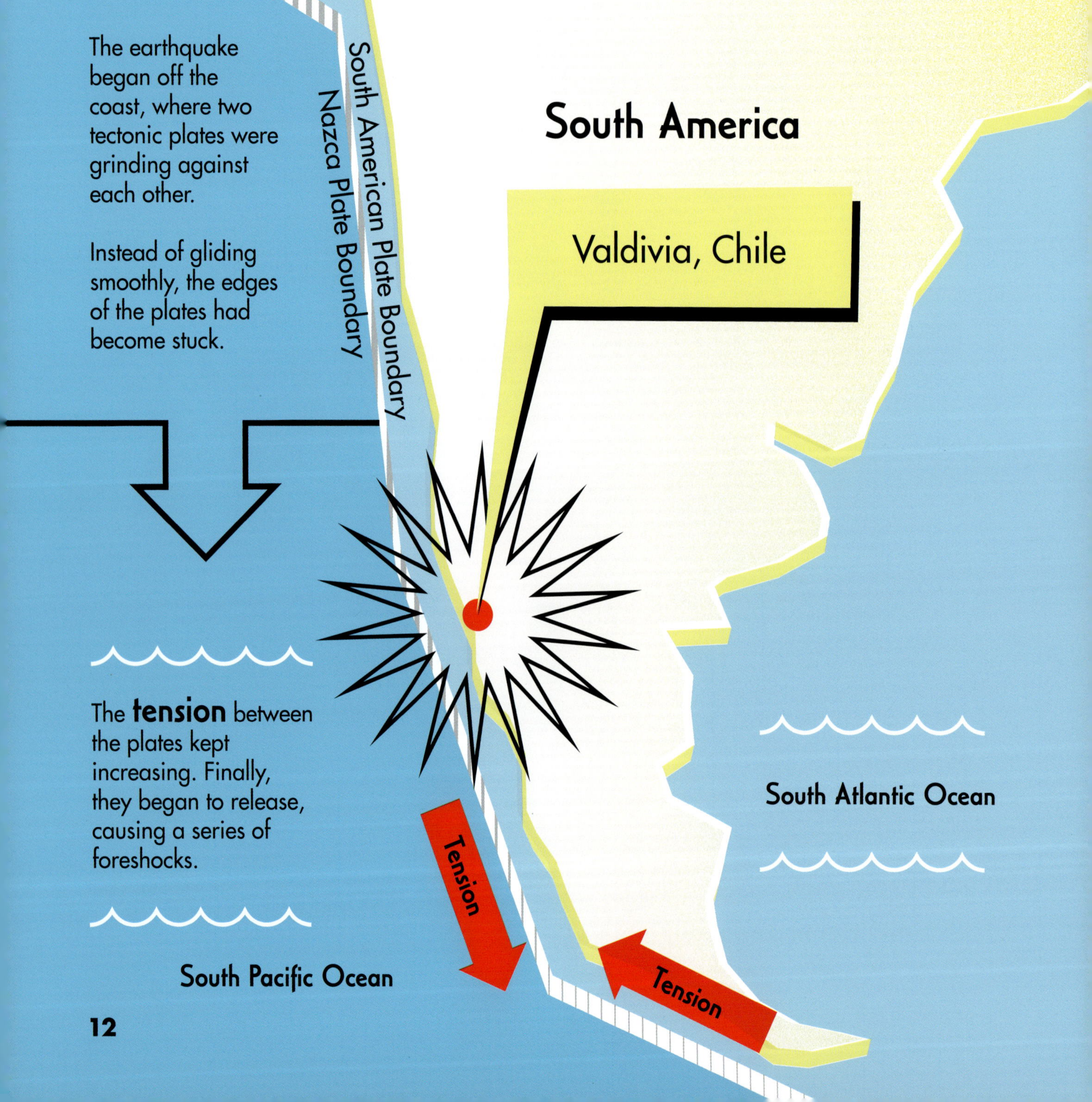

The shockwaves spread out from the epicenter like ripples on a pond. They were felt hundreds of miless away.

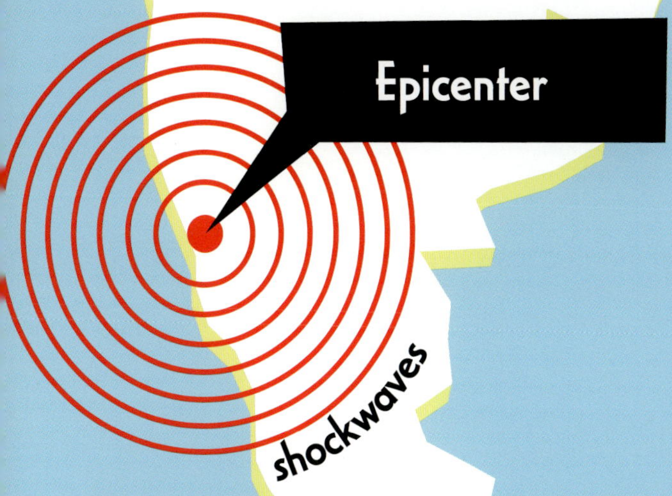

The loosened tectonic plates lurched violently into new positions, causing a giant earthquake.

The foreshocks loosened the plates–like when you hit a stuck jar lid and make it easier to open.

In Chile, thousands of buildings were so badly shaken that they collapsed. Two million people lost their homes. Many people were injured or died.

There were many

landslides.

Whole towns shifted suddenly to the west–by as much as

30 feet (9 m).

Tsunami!

On December 26, 2004, people living or visiting countries along the Indian Ocean noticed the sea level suddenly go down. Some knew what it foretold: a tsunami was coming.

The tsunami began with an earthquake, deep below the ocean.

The waves traveled at over 310 miles (500 km) per hour.

Out in the deep ocean the waves were barely noticeable, less than 3.3 feet (1 m) high.

The pulses were like the waves in a sheet you quickly flap up and down repeatedly.

A 745-mile (1200-km) long section of tectonic plate under the Indian Ocean had suddenly moved. The earthquake pushed up the ocean water above.

Gravity pulled the water down again. This fast rise and fall sent pulses of movement across the ocean.

When the waves reached shallow water, they slowed down. They dragged in extra water from the shore and grew in size.

In some places, the tsunami was **100 feet (30 m)** high when it crashed onto land.

Around the Indian Ocean, the tsunami uprooted trees, smashed houses, and threw boats inland. In total, roughly a quarter of a million people are thought to have died.

Flash Flood!

In Cornwall, UK, summer rain is not unusual. On July 18, 2017, though, it began raining especially hard. Then hailstones big enough to smash windows began to fall.

For the village of Coverack, things were about to get even more extreme. A flash flood was on its way.

The wind blew the storm clouds toward land.

Hours before, thunderstorms had formed over the warm sea. Their warm air contained a lot of **moisture.**

As the storm clouds reached high ground, the storm clouds cooled. Their moisture turned to raindrops and hailstones, then fell.

The water rushed downhill. It flowed down steep valleys toward the coast.

So much rain fell that the river in Coverack could not contain it. Water was soon racing down narrow lanes and streets, and through people's houses.

It tore up roads, knocked down fences and walls, and carried away wooden buildings.

Some people even had to be rescued from the roof of their house by helicopter.

Avalanche!

In Afghanistan in February 2010, avalanches swept across the Salang Pass road to Kabul. More than 160 people were killed.

The avalanches, like almost all others, had been caused by a combination of snow and warm weather.

If the sun comes out and the temperature gets warmer, the top layer of snow melts and becomes water.

As winter begins, **snow falls** on the high mountains.

On the cold ground, the snow does not melt. It piles up wherever the land is flat enough. Sometimes the snow piles up above a steep slope or a cliff.

When night falls and the temperature drops, the watery layer freezes. It turns into ice.

When more snow falls, it lands on slippery ice instead of

grippy ground.

Eventually, so much snow falls that it all slips off the icy layer below.

Avalanche!

The avalanche races down the mountain, collecting more snow as it goes. It also collects mountaineers, trees, ski lifts, skiers, houses–anything in its way.

Hurricane!

On August 26, 2017, Hurricane Harvey hit Texas. Within days, 50 people were dead and there was a trail of destruction wherever Harvey had been.

Harvey, like all hurricanes, had started life over an area of warm ocean water.

As more and more air rushes in, the storm grows increasingly powerful.

By the time it has become a hurricane, it may be about 9 miles (15 km) high and big enough to see from space!

Warm water vapor rises to form clouds. The clouds grow taller and taller.

Down below, more air rushes in to replace the rising air. It swirls around, warming up and rising in its turn.

Hurricane Harvey

Category 1:	**Category 2:**	**Category 3:**	**Category 4:**	**Category 5:**
74–95 mile (119–153 km) per hour winds	96–110 mile (154–177 km) per hour winds	111–129 mile (178–208 km) per hour winds	130–156 miles (209–251 km) per hour winds	155+ mile (252+ km) per hour winds

When a hurricane reaches land, warm ocean water no longer powers the swirl of rising air. It slows down.

The hurricane's giant clouds release their water. Hurricane Harvey dropped over 3 feet (0.9 m) of rain on parts of Texas.

Whole streets became rivers.

Some people took refuge on rooftops.

Others were rescued from their flooded homes.

Water Pressure

For tens of thousands of years, Aboriginal Australians have been traveling across their continent's parched deserts. They survived because they knew about springs where fresh water mysteriously appeared at the surface.

The water's story had begun millions of years ago–when dinosaurs still walked the Earth.

Back then, Australia's sandstone rock was covered by a layer of waterproof rock.

Mountain rain began to sink below ground and into the sandstone. It spread out, but could not rise to the surface. Every time it rained, more water was pushed underground.

Later, an edge of the rock was pushed up by the movement of tectonic plates, forming the Great Dividing Range of mountains.

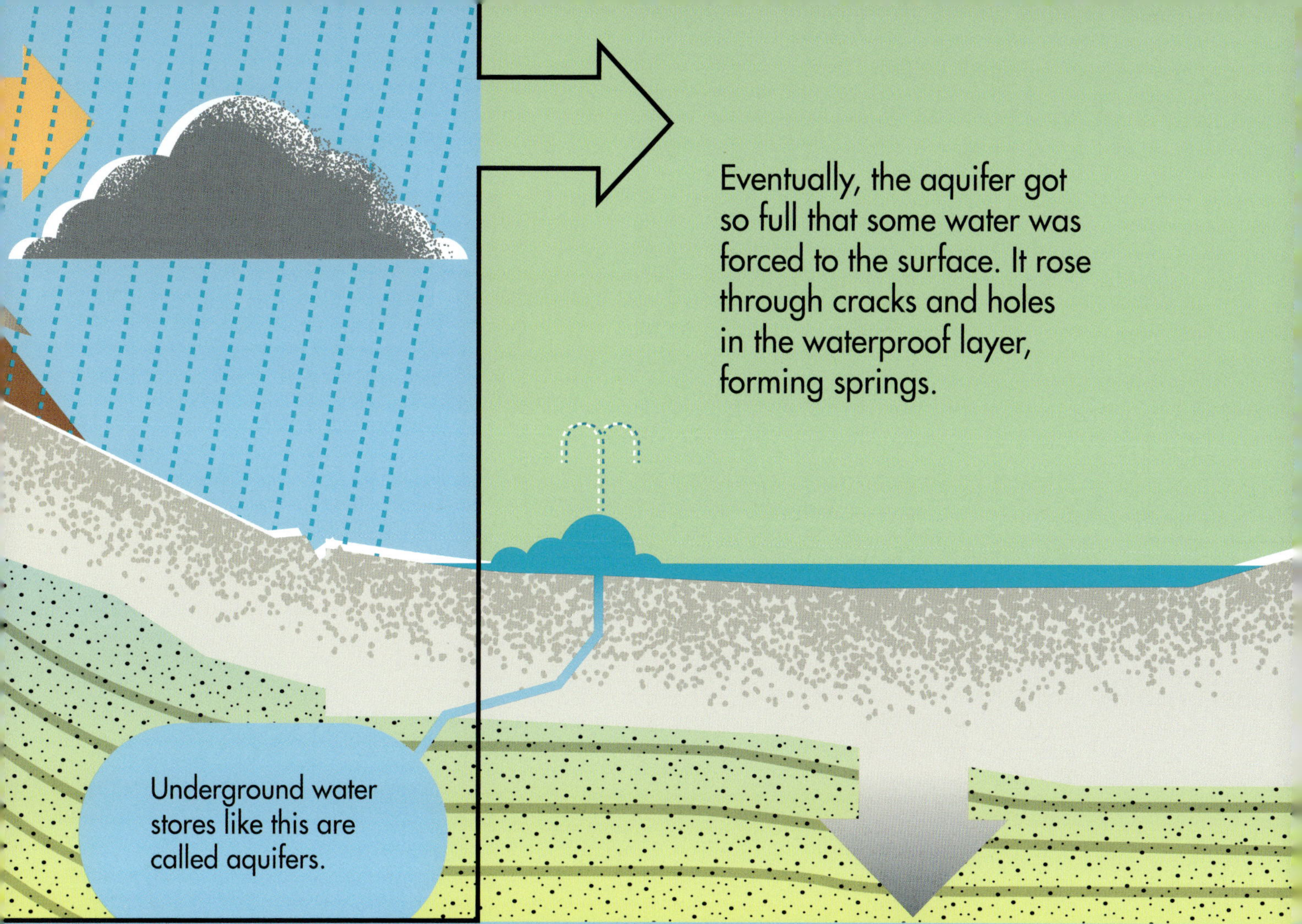

Eventually, the aquifer got so full that some water was forced to the surface. It rose through cracks and holes in the waterproof layer, forming springs.

Underground water stores like this are called aquifers.

Today, aquifers provide water for millions of people. But more water is taken out of them than flows in.

Because of this, wells and springs have started to run dry. Boreholes have to go deeper to reach the water.

Swamps and wetlands have dried up.

This is a disaster for the creatures who live here.

Wildfire!

Almost every year in the United States, thousands of Californians are forced to flee their homes because fires are headed their way. When they return, some find only the smoking shell of their house.

The fires are among thousands that spring up around the world every year.

The heat of summer dries out the plants and soil.

Something starts a fire among the dried-out plants. The flames grow higher and trees begin to catch light.

Wildfires are started by lightning, sparks from rockfalls, dropped cigarettes, barbecues, and a range of other causes.

Wind pushes the fire toward more dried-up vegetation. A line of flames called a "fire front" forms.

Heat from the fire front dries out the trees and plants ahead. They release flammable gases and burst into flame.

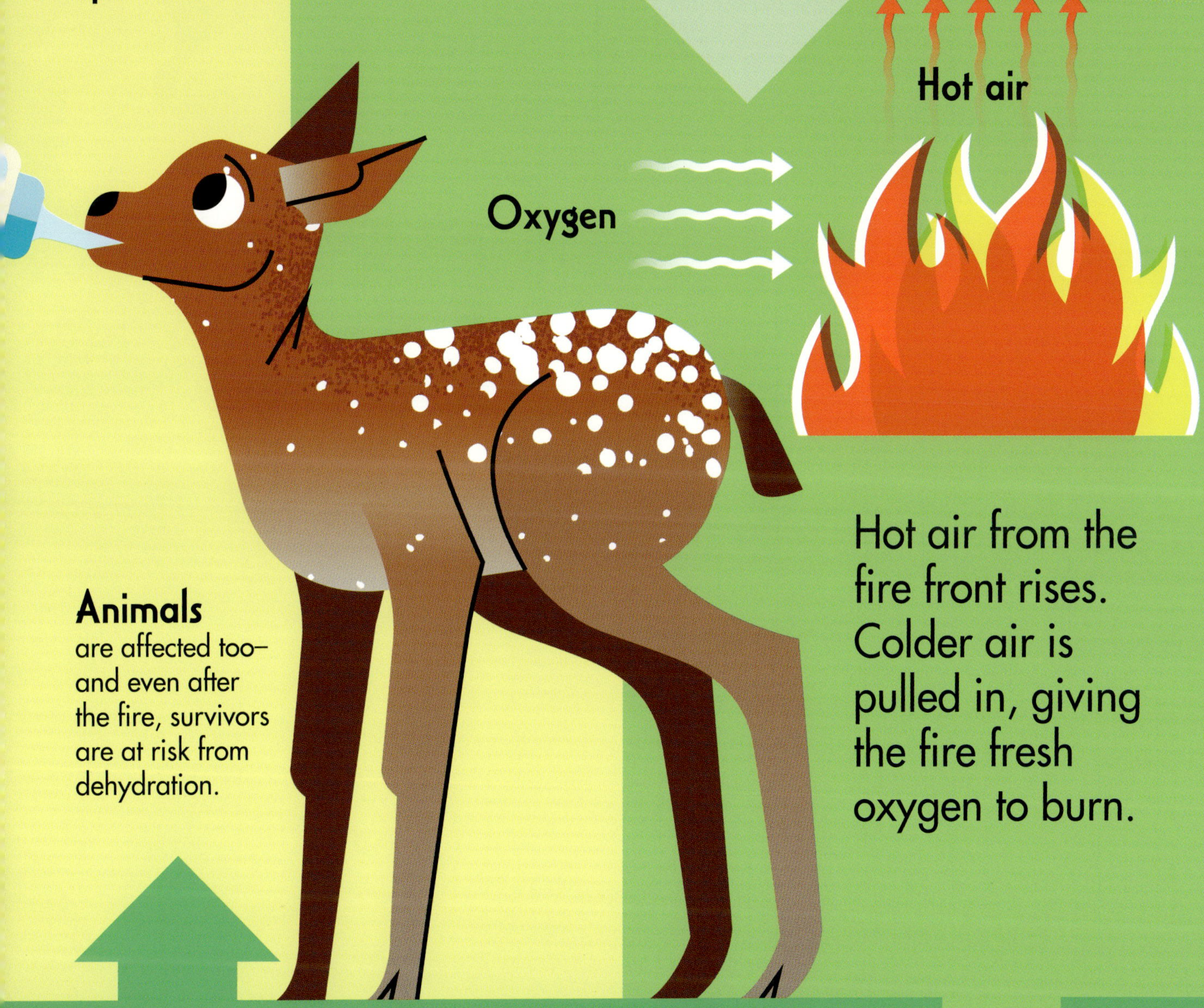

Hot air from the fire front rises. Colder air is pulled in, giving the fire fresh oxygen to burn.

Animals are affected too– and even after the fire, survivors are at risk from dehydration.

Now the fire may rage for weeks. It will destroy thousands of homes, and anyone caught in the fire's path will lose their life.

When the Sea Eats the Land

Lennox Island is off the coast of Canada. Lennox is small–and getting smaller. In 1880, it was 1,520 acres (615 ha). Today it is 1,235 acres (500 ha). Like coasts around the world, Lennox Island is being eaten away in a process called coastal erosion.

Out at sea, a storm appears.

Wind blows across the surface, forming waves.

The longer and stronger the wind blows, the bigger the waves become.

The waves travel toward the shore. When they reach shallow water, they rise up and start to break.

The waves crash against the coast, smashing down rocks and sand.

In places where the land is soft and earthy, it is washed away like a sandcastle in a rising tide.

Where the land is rocky, the water attacks by forcing air into cracks in the rock, making them bigger and splitting the rock.

Air

The land above suddenly has nothing holding it up. It collapses into the sea.

Sometimes lighthouses, gardens, or even people's houses fall into the sea too.

Overheating Earth

Earth is getting warmer. In 2016, the average temperature was 1.69°F (0.9°C) warmer than the average from 1900–2000.

Warmer temperatures may sound like a good thing–but they are actually having a chaotic effect on planet Earth. And what's worse is that humans have caused them.

Between the 1960s and today, the world's population more than doubled.* Industry, agriculture, and other human activity also increased.

Human activities produced gases called greenhouse gases, which were released into the **atmosphere.**

Since 1960, the amount of greenhouse gases we release has gone up by nearly 30 percent.

The greenhouse gases joined a layer high in the sky that traps heat in the atmosphere.

*From roughly 3 billion to 7 billion.

Earth's average air and sea temperatures slowly increased.

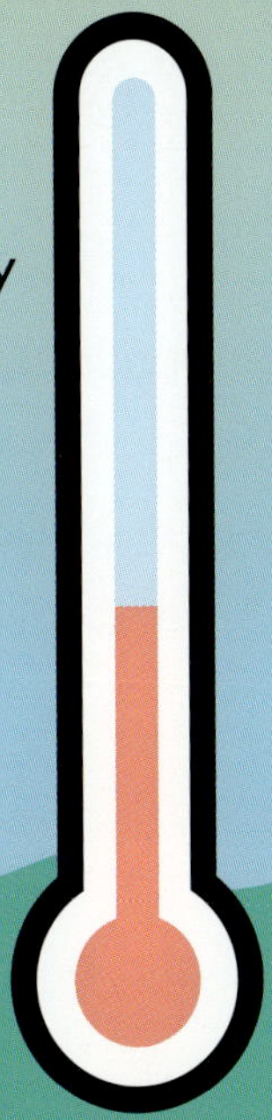

Today this is having **disastrous effects.**

Melting ice caps and glaciers, plus the greater volume of warm water, mean sea levels are rising.

Whole countries may disappear as a result.*

Warmer oceans mean storms and hurricanes happen more often and are more powerful.

Rising air temperatures are causing droughts and increasing the size of deserts around the world.

*Tuvalu, Kiribati, and the Maldives are all in danger of being swamped.

Glossary

Aboriginal Australian descendant of the original peoples of Australia, who lived there before Europeans arrived

accretion in space, the process of matter gathering together in layers to form a planet

active volcano that still erupts regularly

atmosphere layer of gases around a planet

break the moment when the wave pitches forward and becomes frothy and foamy

continent large, continuous area of land. Earth's continents are Africa, Antarctica, Asia, Australia, Europe, North America, and South America.

core center or heart of a round object, for example a planet

epicenter place on Earth's surface directly above where an earthquake happens

flammable able to be easily set alight

glacier large, solid mass of ice, rock, and soil that collects in a steep-sided valley

ice cap large areas of ice at the North and South Poles

magma liquid or semi-liquid rock beneath the Earth's crust

moisture water contained in air

parched dry, without water

spring place where water rises up from beneath the ground

supercell storm rare kind of giant, violent thunderstorm

swamped flooded with water

tectonic plate huge section of rock that makes up part of Earth's outer crust

tension strain or stretch that results from two forces being in opposition to each other

tornado swirling column of air that can pick up large objects, rip off house roofs, and cause lots of damage

volume amount of space something takes up

Finding out more

Books

Henry, Leilani Raashida. *The Call of Antarctica*. Minneapolis, MN: Twenty-First Century Books, 2024.

Wu, Karen Tam. *What a Waste: 9 Ways to Fight Climate Change*. Victoria, BC, Canada: Orca Book Publishers, 2025.

Websites

Earth: NASA Space Place
https://spaceplace.nasa.gov/menu/earth/
Learn more about our planet here.

Earth Science for Kids
https://www.amnh.org/explore/ology/earth
Find out more about the science of our Earth.

Index